First World War
and Army of Occupation
War Diary
France, Belgium and Germany

18 DIVISION
Divisional Troops
15 Motor Machine Gun Battery
24 July 1915 - 31 December 1915

WO95/2028/3

The Naval & Military Press Ltd
www.nmarchive.com
Published in association with The National Archives

Published by

The Naval & Military Press Ltd

Unit 10 Ridgewood Industrial Park,

Uckfield, East Sussex,

TN22 5QE England

Tel: +44 (0) 1825 749494

www.naval-military-press.com

www.nmarchive.com

This diary has been reprinted in facsimile from the original. Any imperfections are inevitably reproduced and the quality may fall short of modern type and cartographic standards.

© **Crown Copyright**
Images reproduced by permission of The National Archives, London, England, 2015.

Contents

Document type	Place/Title	Date From	Date To
Heading	WO95/2028/3		
Heading	18th Divisional Troops. 15th M.M. Gun Battery. July-Dec 1915.		
Heading	Motor Machine Gun Service R.F.A. 15th Battery. Capt. J. Joyce. Comdg. Formed at Bisley May. 29th 1915. Attached 18th Division. July 22nd 1915. 10th Corps. 3rd Army. Vol I		
War Diary		24/07/1915	29/07/1915
War Diary	Flesselles	01/08/1915	31/08/1915
War Diary	Flesselles	06/08/1915	22/08/1915
War Diary	Ribemont	01/09/1915	31/12/1915

WO 95/20287 (3)

WO 95/20287 (3)

18th DIVISIONAL TROOPS.

15TH H.M. GUN BATTERY.

JULY - DEC 1915.

18 DIV TPS
BEF

ORBAT
1915 AUG & DEC 18 DIV

Motor Machine Gun Service R.F.A.

15th Battery. Capt. J. Joyce. comdg.

Formed at Bisley May. 29th 1915.

Attached 18th Division. July. 22nd 1915.

10th Corps. 3rd Army.

Vol I

July 1915 — Dec 1915

15th By Motor Machine Gun Service

WAR DIARY or INTELLIGENCE SUMMARY

Army Form C. 2118

Place	Date	Hour	Summary of Events and Information	Remarks and references to Appendices
July	24		Embarked for France from Southampton	
	25		Disembarked Havre	
	28		Abbeville	
	29		Flexicourt	

15TH BATTERY MOTOR MACHINE GUN SERVICE
CAPTAIN COMDG

15th By Motor Machine Gun Service

WAR DIARY or INTELLIGENCE SUMMARY

Army Form C. 2118

Place	Date	Hour	Summary of Events and Information	Remarks and references to Appendices
Aug. Hazebles	1/31		Training	
	6/7		St. Omer (Wisagnes M.G. School). Battery inspected by F.M. Gen French	
	8		St Gratien	
	21		Morlancourt	
	22		Ville-sur-Ancre	

Army Form C. 2118

WAR DIARY
or
INTELLIGENCE SUMMARY
(Erase heading not required.)

Instructions regarding War Diaries and Intelligence Summaries are contained in F.S. Regs., Part II. and the Staff Manual respectively. Title Pages will be prepared in manuscript.

Places	Date	Hour	Summary of Events and Information	Remarks and references to Appendices
Sept	1		Sections in trenches D.1. D.2. D.3 for instruction	
Ribemont	8		No 3 section engaged with enemy 12 midnight - 5 a.m in Bois Francais Co-operating with 11th Royal Fusiliers. The guns were used to hold crater of mine and to repel Counter-attack by the enemy. Casualties 2 wounded, 1 officer, 1 n.c.o.	
	18/9		Ribemont. Training with Divisional Mounted Troops.	

15th Motor Machine Gun Service

Army Form C. 2118

WAR DIARY
or
INTELLIGENCE SUMMARY
(Erase heading not required.)

Instructions regarding War Diaries and Intelligence Summaries are contained in F. S. Regs., Part. II. and the Staff Manual respectively. Title Pages will be prepared in manuscript.

Place	Date	Hour	Summary of Events and Information	Remarks and references to Appendices
October	1/31		Training with Divisional Mounted Troops	
Rivemont	16/31		Instruct 53 Brigade Machine Gun Section on Vickers M. G.	

15th By Motor Machine Gun Serv.

Army Form C. 2118

WAR DIARY
or
INTELLIGENCE SUMMARY

Place	Date	Hour	Summary of Events and Information	Remarks and references to Appendices
November	1/18		Continue instruction of classes.	
Rivemont	12/31		All sections engaged along Divisional line in indirect fire. The objectives, all roads within range of 3,000 yards used by the enemy for transport. Intelligence summaries show enemy transport dislocated as a result	

15th By Motor Machine GunService

WAR DIARY
or
INTELLIGENCE SUMMARY

Army Form C. 2118

Place	Date	Hour	Summary of Events and Information	Remarks and references to Appendices
December	1/25.		Indirect fire continued. Casualties. 3 wounded (Gunners)	
Ribemont.	26.	11:30am	Co-operate with x corp Artillery in bombardment of Tricourt	
"	26/31		Sections engaged in keeping open breaches in enemy defences caused by Artillery bombardment.	